LPR COOKBOOK

MAIN COURSE – 80+ Easy recipes designed to reduce stomach acid naturally and gastritis relief (GERD & Acid reflux effective approach)

TABLE OF CONTENTS

- PANCAKES 6
- POTATO PANCAKES WITH PROSCIUTTO...7
- LEMON AND RAISIN PANCAKES 8
- AMERICAN PANCAKES...9
- COCONUT OATS 10
- STRAWBERRY OATS 11
- OVERNIGHT OATS..12
- FRIED EGGS..13
- SCRAMBLED EGGS 14
- CRISPY BACON 15
- FRENCH TOAST 16
- COCONUT OMELETTE 17
- BANANA BREAKFAST CHEESECAKE...18
- BANANA BREAKFAST MUFFINS 19
- BANANA SMOOTHIE..20
- PEANUT BUTTER & MINT SMOOTHIE..21
- SUMMER SMOOTHIE..22
- CHOCOLATE BREAKFAST SMOOTHIE...23
- CHOCOLATE BREAKFAST CHEESECAKE SMOOTHIE 24
- STRAWBERRY BREAKFAST SMOOTHIE 25
- ALMOND BREAKFAST SMOOTHIE..26
- BEEF STEW..27
- BORSCHT 29
- ROAST..30
- BUTTERNUT SQUASH SOUP 31
- CANNELLINI BEAN SOUP 32
- CHICKEN TORTILLA SOUP 33
- BLACK EYED PEA SOUP 35
- BLACK EYED PEA SOUP – COUMADIN SAFE...36
- PEA SOUP WITH HERBS..37

PEA SOUP WITH HERBS – LOW SODIUM	38
CHILLED WATERMELON SOUP	39
POTATO SOUP	40
FAVA BEAN SOUP	41
FAVA BEAN SOUP – LOW SODIUM	42
EGGPLANT & GARLIC SOUP	43
FISH SOUP WITH YAMS	44
CUCUMBER SOUP	46
CHICKPEA SOUP	47
LENTIL CHILI	49
POTAGE A LA FLORENTINE	51
CHICKEN NOODLE SOUP	52
CHICKEN NOODLE SOUP – COUMADIN SAFE	54
ROASTED EGGPLANT SOUP	56
ROASTED TOMATO SOUP WITH GARLIC	58
ROASTED YAM SOUP	60
ROASTED YAM SOUP – LOW SODIUM	62
BEAN SOUP	64
WHITE BEAN SOUP	65
WHITE BEAN SOUP WITH KALE	66
WHITE BEAN CHILI	68
CHICKEN WONTON SOUP	70
HOMEMADE CHICKEN NUGGETS	72
ROASTED VEGGIE BREAKFAST TACOS	73
PUDDING WITH HONEYDEW MELON	74
ROASTED VEGGIE WITH CHEESE	75
SWEET POTATO WITH GINGER-HONEY ALMOND BUTTER	76
APPLE CARROT MUFFINS	77
DRIED PERSIMMON ROUNDS	79
PAPAYA YOGURT	80
BERRY ICE CUBES WITH SELTZER	81
DIY BAGELS	82

GRILLED VEGETABLES 84

APPLE CRISP DESSET 85

BUTTERMILK RANCH DRESSING 87

PESTO AND BUTTERNUT SQUASH PIZZA 88

CRISPY FRENCH FRIES 90

MANGO COLESLAW 91

CHICKEN WITH TURMERIC 92

WILD BLUEBERRY MUFFINS 93

QUINOA SALAD 94

OVERNIGHT OATMEAL 95

AVOCADO CHICKEN SALAD 96

BASIL FARRO SALAD 97

STRAWBERRY ICE CUBES 98

LEMON ZUCCHINI SALAD 99

SPICED CHICKEN AND VEGETABLE SOUP 100

QUINOA STUFFED CHICKEN ROLL-UPS 101

TURKEY AND MUSHROOM BURGERS 103

LEMON-ZESTED SHRIMP 104

COD PARCHMENT PACKS 105

PANCACKES WITH RED APPLES 106

CHICKEN SOUP NOODLE BOWL 108

Copyright 2018 by Noah Jerris - All rights reserved.

This document is geared towards providing exact and reliable information in regards to the topic and issue covered. The publication is sold with the idea that the publisher is not required to render accounting, officially permitted, or otherwise, qualified services. If advice is necessary, legal or professional, a practiced individual in the profession should be ordered.

- From a Declaration of Principles which was accepted and approved equally by a Committee of the American Bar Association and a Committee of Publishers and Associations.

In no way is it legal to reproduce, duplicate, or transmit any part of this document in either electronic means or in printed format. Recording of this publication is strictly prohibited and any storage of this document is not allowed unless with written permission from the publisher. All rights reserved.

The information provided herein is stated to be truthful and consistent, in that any liability, in terms of inattention or otherwise, by any usage or abuse of any policies, processes, or directions contained within is the solitary and utter responsibility of the recipient reader. Under no circumstances will any legal responsibility or blame be held against the publisher for any reparation, damages, or monetary loss due to the information herein, either directly or indirectly.

Respective authors own all copyrights not held by the publisher.

The information herein is offered for informational purposes solely, and is universal as so. The presentation of the information is without contract or any type of guarantee assurance.

The trademarks that are used are without any consent, and the publication of the trademark is without permission or backing by the trademark owner. All trademarks and brands within this book are for clarifying purposes only and are the owned by the owners themselves, not affiliated with this document.

Introduction

LPR recipes for family and personal enjoyment. You will love them for how easy it is to prepare them.

PANCAKES

Serves: 2

Prep Time: 10 Minutes

Cook Time: 20 Minutes

Total Time: 30 Minutes

INGREDIENTS

- 1 egg
- 100 g plain flour
- ¼ tsp salt
- olive oil
- 350 ml milk

DIRECTIONS

1. In a bowl sift the flour and the salt
2. Add the egg and beat it it with the flour and salt
3. Add 70ml of the milk and whisk together
4. Add the remaining milk and whisk will adding
5. In a pan add olive olive over low heat and increase heat gradually
6. Pour the mixture into the pan and cook for 1-2 minutes each side
7. Repeat the process and serve when ready

POTATO PANCAKES WITH PROSCIUTTO

Serves: *4*

Prep Time: *10* Minutes

Cook Time: *20* Minutes

Total Time: *30* Minutes

INGREDIENTS

- 35g cheese
- 350g mashed potato
- 2 eggs
- 200g flour
- 250 milk
- ¼ tsp salt

DIRECTIONS

1. In a bowl add the mashed potato, milk and flour and whisk together
2. Place a frying pan over low heat and pour the mixture in the pan
3. Sprinkle some cheese over the pancake
4. Cook for 1-2 minutes on each side
5. Serve with Prosciutto between each pancake

LEMON AND RAISIN PANCAKES

Serves: **4**

Prep Time: **10** Minutes

Cook Time: **15** Minutes

Total Time: **25** Minutes

INGREDIENTS

- 150g raising flour
- 45 sugar
- 250 milk
- 2 eggs
- zest of 3 lemons
- 100g raisins

DIRECTIONS

1. **In a bowl mix the raising flour with sugar**
2. **In another bowl beat the eggs and add milk and whisk until smooth**
3. **Add the egg and milk mixture into the first bowl, zest the lemons and whisk**
4. **Place a frying pan over medium heat and pour the mixture**
5. **Over each pancake sprinkle raisins and cook on each side**

AMERICAN PANCAKES

Serves: **4**

Prep Time: **10** Minutes

Cook Time: **10** Minutes

Total Time: **20** Minutes

INGREDIENTS

- 220g self raising flour
- 50g sugar
- 2 eggs

DIRECTIONS

1. In a bowl mix sugar with self raising flour
2. Add 2 eggs and beat them with the mixture
3. Add milk gradually into the mixture and whisk together
4. Place a frying pan over medium heat and pour the mixture into the pan
5. Cook each pancake for 1-2 minutes per side

COCONUT OATS

Serves: *1*

Prep Time: *10* Minutes

Cook Time: *5* Minutes

Total Time: *15* Minutes

INGREDIENTS

- 50g oats
- 15g desiccated coconut
- 1 tsp cocoa powder
- 100 coconut milk
- 1 tsp almonds

DIRECTIONS

1. Place the cocoa powder, pots, coconut milk, desiccated coconut in a bowl and stir
2. Cover and and add to the fridge over night
3. Serve in the morning with flaked almonds

STRAWBERRY OATS

Serves: *1*

Prep Time: *10* Minutes

Cook Time: *10* Minutes

Total Time: *20* Minutes

INGREDIENTS

- 50g oats
- 1 tablespoon nuts
- 30g strawberries
- 100 almond milk
- 2 tsp maple syrup

DIRECTIONS

1. In a bowl add the oats and almond milk and cover them, put in the fridge over night
2. Next day add strawberries over the oats, also add nuts and maple syrup
3. Serve when ready!

OVERNIGHT OATS

Serves: *1*

Prep Time: *5* Minutes

Cook Time: *5* Minutes

Total Time: *10* Minutes

INGREDIENTS

- 50g oats
- 150 skimmed milk

DIRECTIONS

1. In a bowl add oats and milk and cover them
2. Place them in the fridge overnight
3. Next morning serve with topping

FRIED EGGS

Serves: 5

Prep Time: 5   Minutes

Cook Time: 10 Minutes

Total Time: 15 Minutes

INGREDIENTS

- 1 eggs
- olive oil
- salt

DIRECTIONS

1. Add olive oil in a frying pan over medium heat
2. Crack the egg in the pan and cook for a couple of minutes each side
3. Remove and serve with salt or pepper

SCRAMBLED EGGS

Serves: 2

Prep Time: **10** Minutes

Cook Time: **10** Minutes

Total Time: **20** Minutes

INGREDIENTS

- 2 eggs
- 50 ml fat milk
- 1 tsp butter
- ¼ tablespoons salt

DIRECTIONS

1. In a bowl the eggs with some milk and season with salt
2. Place a pan over medium heat and add olive oil
3. Pour the mixture in the pan and cook for 1-2 minutes each side
4. Remove and serve!

CRISPY BACON

Serves: *1*

Prep Time: *10* Minutes

Cook Time: *20* Minutes

Total Time: *30* Minutes

INGREDIENTS

- Streaky bacon

DIRECTIONS

1. **Preheat the oven to 375 F**
2. **In a baking tray put ley out the bacon and cook for 15-20 minutes**
3. **When the bacon is crispy remove and serve**

FRENCH TOAST

Serves: 2

Prep Time: 10 Minutes

Cook Time: 10 Minutes

Total Time: 20 Minutes

INGREDIENTS

- 2 eggs
- zest of ½ orange
- butter
- 2 tablespoons milk
- 10 slices fruit bread

DIRECTIONS

1. In a bowl mix eggs, orange zest and eggs, beat the eggs before and mix everything together
2. Place a slice of bread into the mixture to soak
3. Place a pan over medium heat
4. Place the bread slices in the pan and cook for 1-2 minutes on each side
5. Remove and serve with maple syrup

COCONUT OMELETTE

Serves: **4**

Prep Time: **10** Minutes

Cook Time: **10** Minutes

Total Time: **20** Minutes

INGREDIENTS

- 2 eggs
- ½ tsp honey
- 1 tsp coconut oil

DIRECTIONS

1. In a bowl beat 2 eggs, add honey and stir
2. In a frying pan heat coconut oil over medium heat and pour the mixture
3. Cook on each side for 1-2 minutes
4. Remove and serve with salt or pepper

BANANA BREAKFAST CHEESECAKE

Serves: *1*

Prep Time: *10* Minutes

Cook Time: *10* Minutes

Total Time: *20* Minutes

INGREDIENTS

- 2 tsp chocolate chips
- vanilla extract
- 1 tsp almond butter
- 1 tsp honey
- 2 tablespoons oats
- 1 tablespoon cream cheese
- 1 banana

DIRECTIONS

1. **In a bowl mix almond butter, oats and honey**
2. **Slice a banana and add it to the mixture**
3. **In the microwave add chocolate chips for 1 minute, add vanilla extract and cream cheese to the melted chocolate**
4. **Top the banana with chocolate mixture and serve**

BANANA BREAKFAST MUFFINS

Serves: 2
Prep Time: *10* Minutes
Cook Time: *30* Minutes
Total Time: *40* Minutes

INGREDIENTS

- 50 flour
- 30 wheat germ
- 1 egg
- 120 ml milk
- 5 muffin cases
- 100g oats
- 50g honey
- ½ tablespoons baking powder
- 1 tsp salt
- 1 banana

DIRECTIONS

1. Preheat oven to 325 F and place a muffin case into a muffin tin
2. In a bowl add baking powder, salt, flour and a mashed banana
3. Add oats, wheat germ and stir everything together
4. Add he remaining ingredients and stir until everything is mixed
5. Scoop the mixture into the muffin cases and place them in the oven for 20-25 minutes
6. When ready remove and serve

BANANA SMOOTHIE

Serves: **1**

Prep Time: **10** Minutes

Cook Time: **10** Minutes

Total Time: **20** Minutes

INGREDIENTS

- 1 banana
- 1 shot of expresso
- 200 ml milk
- 1 tablespoon oats

DIRECTIONS

1. In a blender add the ingredients and blend until smooth
2. When ready add a handful of ice cubes and blend
3. When ready remove and serve

PEANUT BUTTER & MINT SMOOTHIE

Serves: **1**

Prep Time: **10** Minutes

Cook Time: **30** Minutes

Total Time: **40** Minutes

INGREDIENTS

- 220 ml almond milk
- 40g fresh spinach
- 1 tsp peanut butter
- mint leaves
- 1 banana

DIRECTIONS

1. **In a blender add all the ingredients and blend until smooth**
2. **When ready remove and serve**

SUMMER SMOOTHIE

Serves: *1*

Prep Time: *10* Minutes

Cook Time: *10* Minutes

Total Time: *20* Minutes

INGREDIENTS

- 220 ml coconut milk
- 50g frozen mango
- 50 g frozen pineapple
- 1 banana

DIRECTIONS

1. **In a blender add all the ingredients and blend until smooth**
2. **When ready remove and serve**

CHOCOLATE BREAKFAST SMOOTHIE

Serves: **1**

Prep Time: **10** Minutes

Cook Time: **10** Minutes

Total Time: **20** Minutes

INGREDIENTS

- 1 banana
- 1 tablespoon oats
- vanilla extract
- 220 coconut milk
- 1 tsp cacao powder

DIRECTIONS

1. **In a blender add all the ingredients and blend until smooth**
2. **When ready remove and serve**

CHOCOLATE BREAKFAST CHEESECAKE SMOOTHIE

Serves: *1*

Prep Time: *5* Minutes

Cook Time: *5* Minutes

Total Time: *10* Minutes

INGREDIENTS

- 1 banana
- 1 tsp cream cheese
- 1 tsp dark chocolate chips
- 1 tsp almond butter
- 220 skimmed milk
- 1 tablespoon oats

DIRECTIONS

1. **In a blender add all the ingredients and blend until smooth**
2. **When ready remove and serve**

STRAWBERRY BREAKFAST SMOOTHIE

Serves: 2

Prep Time: 5 Minutes

Cook Time: 10 Minutes

Total Time: 15 Minutes

INGREDIENTS

- 350 ml skimmed milk
- 6 strawberries
- 2 tablespoons wheat germ
- 1 banana

DIRECTIONS

1. **In a blender add all the ingredients and blend until smooth**
2. **When ready remove and serve**

ALMOND BREAKFAST SMOOTHIE

Serves: *1*

Prep Time: *5* Minutes

Cook Time: *5* Minutes

Total Time: *10* Minutes

INGREDIENTS

- 1 banana
- 1 tsp almond butter
- 2 tablespoons oats
- 220 ml skimmed milk

DIRECTIONS

1. **In a blender add all the ingredients and blend until smooth**
2. **When ready remove and serve**

SOUP

BEEF STEW

Serves: **4**

Prep Time: **10** Minutes

Cook Time: **80** Minutes

Total Time: **90** Minutes

INGREDIENTS

- 3 cups water
- 20 pearl onions
- 2 bay leaves
- 1 1/2 lbs. potatoes
- ¼ ground all spice
- 1/3 cup white flour
- 1 tsp salt
- ¼ tsp black pepper
- 1 ½ lbs. flank steak
- ½ mushrooms
- 1 tablespoons lemon juice
- 1 tablespoons sauce
- 1 lb. carrots

DIRECTIONS

1. In a stock pot add water and heat place it over high heat

2. Add onions and cook them for 10 minutes
3. Preheat oven to 400 F
4. In a paper ag mix pepper, flour and salt and toss the flank steak in the mixture
5. Add the flank steak in a skillet and cook until brown
6. Remove the meat and add onions to the skillet
7. Add everything to the stock pot, in the skillet add the sauce and the lemon juice and deglaze the pan
8. Add the carrots, bay leaves, all spice and potatoes to the oven
9. Cook for one hour and stir frequently

BORSCHT

Serves: **6**

Prep Time: **10** Minutes

Cook Time: **160** Minutes

Total Time: **170** Minutes

INGREDIENTS

- 3 lb beets
- 1 tsp olive oil
- ¼ tsp salt
- black pepper
- 1 white onion
- 4 cups water
- ½ lemon
- 6 tablespoons sour cream
- 12 tsp fresh dill

DIRECTIONS

1. Wrap the beets in an aluminum foil and place them in a oven to 300 F
2. Roast for 50-60 minutes and remove to cool
3. In a sauce pan add olive oil over medium heat and add onions to cook for 5-10 minutes
4. Add the peeled beets into the sauce pan with water, pepper, salt and lemon juice
5. Reduce the heat and cook for 50-60 minutes by stirring frequently
6. When soup is ready let it cool, add sour cream and fresh dill to each serving

ROAST

Serves: **4**

Prep Time: **10** Minutes

Cook Time: **50** Minutes

Total Time: **60** Minutes

INGREDIENTS

- 1 ½ lbs. broccoli
- 2 cups milk
- ¼ tsp salt
- 6-ounces cheddar cheese
- 3 cups water
- 2 tsp olive oil
- ½ white onions
- 3 tablespoons white flour

DIRECTIONS

1. In a stock pot add the broccoli with the water and cook on medium heat for 30 minutes and then reduce the heat
2. When the steams are soft, puree them in a blender
3. In the stock pot add olive oil, flour and stir frequently
4. Add milk and stir while the soup thickens
5. When ready remove and serve

BUTTERNUT SQUASH SOUP

Serves: **4**

Prep Time: **10** Minutes

Cook Time: **50** Minutes

Total Time: **60** Minutes

INGREDIENTS

- 3 cups water
- black pepper
- ¼ tsp dried thyme leaves
- ¼ ground nutmeg
- 2 ½ lbs. butternut squash
- ¼ tsp salt

DIRECTIONS

1. In a sauce pan add water over high heat
2. Add the cubed squash in a steamer basket for 20-25 minutes
3. Use a blender to puree the squash until smooth
4. Place the pan over medium heat and add salt, thyme leaves, pepper and ground nutmeg
5. Sit in the remaining water, when ready remove and serve

CANNELLINI BEAN SOUP

Serves: **4**

Prep Time: **10** Minutes

Cook Time: **50** Minutes

Total Time: **60** Minutes

INGREDIENTS

- 2 cups cannellini beans
- 4-quarts water
- 2 tsp olive oil
- 2 cloves garlic
- 1 white onion
- 3 cups chicken
- 1/6 tsp salt
- 2 ribs celery
- 1 tablespoons oregano

DIRECTIONS

1. In a pot place the beans and cover with water
2. Drain the beans next days and place over medium heat
3. Let it boil and reduce the heat for an hour
4. In the pot add olive oil, white onion and garlic
5. Cook and add the beans to the pot and stir
6. Add the chicken and cook for 10-15 minutes, add the celery, black pepper and oregano
7. Cook for another 10-15 minutes

CHICKEN TORTILLA SOUP

Serves: **4**
Prep Time: **10**   Minutes
Cook Time: **50**   Minutes
Total Time: **60**   Minutes

INGREDIENTS

- 2 tsp olive oil
- 1 onion
- 1 tsp ground cumin
- 1 tsp paprika
- 2 tsp chili powder
- 5 cups water
- black pepper
- 18 tortilla chips
- 3 ribs celery
- 1 carrots
- 2 ears corn
- 1 1/2 lb chicken thighs

DIRECTIONS

1. In a stock pot place olive oil over medium heat
2. Add onion and cook for 4-5 minutes, add carrots, celery and cook for another 4-5 minutes
3. Add the chicken, cumin, paprika, water, pepper and chili powder and cook for 2-3 minutes

4. Reduce the heat and cook for 40-45 minutes, stir frequently
5. Serve with crumbled tortilla chips

BLACK EYED PEA SOUP

Serves: *4*

Prep Time: *10* Minutes

Cook Time: *50* Minutes

Total Time: *60* Minutes

INGREDIENTS

- 2 tsp olive oil
- 1 red onion
- black pepper
- 3 cups chicken
- 3 cups water
- 2 16-ounce can black eyed peas
- 8-ounces spinach
- 3 ribs celery
- 1 ½ chicken thighs
- 1 tsp dried sage
- ¼ dried thyme
- ¼ tsp salt

DIRECTIONS

1. In a sauce pan add olive oil over medium heat
2. Add celery and onion and cook for 5-6 minutes
3. Add the thyme, sage and chicken thighs and cook for 5-6 minutes
4. Add pepper, salt, chicken stock black eyed peas and water
5. Cook for 40-45 minutes and stir frequently

BLACK EYED PEA SOUP – COUMADIN SAFE

Serves: **4**

Prep Time: **10** Minutes

Cook Time: **50** Minutes

Total Time: **60** Minutes

INGREDIENTS

- 2 tsp olive oil
- 1 red onion
- black pepper
- 3 cups chicken
- 3 cups water
- 2 16-ounce can black eyed peas
- 8-ounces spinach
- 3 ribs celery
- 1 ½ chicken thighs
- 1 tsp dried sage
- ¼ dried thyme
- ¼ tsp salt

DIRECTIONS

1. In a sauce pan add olive oil over medium heat
2. Add celery and onion and cook for 5-6 minutes
3. Add the thyme, sage and chicken thighs and cook for 5-6 minutes
4. Add pepper, salt, chicken stock black eyed peas and water
5. Cook for 40-45 minutes and stir frequently

PEA SOUP WITH HERBS

Serves: 4

Prep Time: 10   Minutes

Cook Time: 80   Minutes

Total Time: 90   Minutes

INGREDIENTS

- 2 tablespoons olive oil
- 1 large onion
- 2 ½ cups chicken
- 1 tablespoons tarragon
- 2 tablespoons parsley
- ½ chives
- ¼ mint
- 2-ounces goat cheese
- 1 lb. frozen peas
- 1 cup spinach

DIRECTIONS

1. In a bowl add ice
2. In a sauce pan add olive oil over medium heat and add the onions
3. Cook for 5-10 minutes, add the chicken and the peas
4. Stir frequently and cook for another 5-10 minutes
5. Add spinach and cook for 3-4 minutes
6. When ready place the pan in the ice bowl, add tarragon, parley, pepper, salt and goat cheese

PEA SOUP WITH HERBS – LOW SODIUM

Serves: **4**

Prep Time: **10** Minutes

Cook Time: **80** Minutes

Total Time: **90** Minutes

INGREDIENTS

- 2 tablespoons olive oil
- 1 large onion
- 2 ½ cups chicken
- 1 tablespoons tarragon
- 2 tablespoons parsley
- ½ chives
- 2-ounces goat cheese
- 1 lb. frozen peas
- 1 cup spinach

DIRECTIONS

1. In a bowl add ice
2. In a sauce pan add olive oil over medium heat and add the onions
3. Cook for 5-10 minutes, add the chicken and the peas
4. Stir frequently and cook for another 5-10 minutes
5. Add spinach and cook for 3-4 minutes
6. When ready place the pan in the ice bowl, add tarragon, parley, pepper and goat cheese

CHILLED WATERMELON SOUP

Serves: **4**

Prep Time: **10** Minutes

Cook Time: **30** Minutes

Total Time: **40** Minutes

INGREDIENTS

- 3 cups watermelon
- 1 lb. tomatoes
- 3 tablespoons lime juice
- ½ red pepper
- ½ tsp salt
- black pepper
- 3 tsp olive oil
- 6 leaves basil

DIRECTIONS

1. In a blender place the lime juice, red pepper, tomatoes, watermelon, salt and pepper
2. Pour the mixture into a pitcher and place it in a freezer
3. Serve with 1 teaspoon of olive oil and basil leaves

POTATO SOUP

Serves: **4**

Prep Time: **10** Minutes

Cook Time: **30** Minutes

Total Time: **40** Minutes

INGREDIENTS

- 2 tsp olive oil
- ½ cup milk
- black pepper
- 3-ounces cheddar cheese
- 1 green onion
- 1 while onion
- 4 cups water
- 1 lb. potatoes

DIRECTIONS

1. In a saucepan add olive oil over medium heat
2. Add the onion and cook for 4-5 minutes
3. Add the water and potatoes and stir, increase the heat and let it boil
4. Stir frequently for next 20-25 minutes
5. When ready, remove from heat and let it cool, add milk and pepper
6. Serve in bowls with cheddar cheese and green onions

FAVA BEAN SOUP

Serves: **4**

Prep Time: **10** Minutes

Cook Time: **30** Minutes

Total Time: **40** Minutes

INGREDIENTS

- 2 small onions
- 1 carrot
- 6 cups water
- ¼ tsp salt
- black pepper 3 leaves basil
- 2 ounces Parmigiano-Reggiano
- 1 lb. red potatoes
- 14-ounces fava beans
- 1 clove garlic

DIRECTIONS

1. In a sauce pan add all the ingredients
2. Place the pan oven medium heat and let it boil, reduce the heat and simmer for 20-25 minutes
3. When ready serve with Parmigiano and basil

FAVA BEAN SOUP – LOW SODIUM

Serves: **4**

Prep Time: **10** Minutes

Cook Time: **30** Minutes

Total Time: **40** Minutes

INGREDIENTS

- black pepper 3 leaves basil
- 2 ounces Parmigiano-Reggiano
- 1 lb. red potatoes
- 14-ounces fava beans
- 2 small onions
- 1 carrot
- 6 cups water
- 1 clove garlic

DIRECTIONS

1. In a sauce pan add all the ingredients
2. Place the pan oven medium heat and let it boil, reduce the heat and simmer for 20-25 minutes
3. When ready serve with Parmigiano and basil

EGGPLANT & GARLIC SOUP

Serves: **4**

Prep Time: **10** Minutes

Cook Time: **50** Minutes

Total Time: **60** Minutes

INGREDIENTS

- 1 tablespoon olive oil
- black pepper
- 2-ounces goat cheese
- 1 cup water
- 1 15-ounce can white beans
- 22-ounces eggplant
- 1 bulb garlic
- ¼ tsp salt

DIRECTIONS

1. **Preheat the oven to 300 F**
2. **In a skillet add the eggplant and it in the oven**
3. **Add garlic and olive oil to the skillet**
4. **Roast the eggplant with garlic for 30-40 minutes**
5. **Remove and let it cool for 5-10 minutes**
6. **Scoop the meat of the eggplant and place it in a blender, blend until smooth**
7. **Serve when ready**

FISH SOUP WITH YAMS

Serves: **4**

Prep Time: **10** Minutes

Cook Time: **60** Minutes

Total Time: **70** Minutes

INGREDIENTS

- 2 tablespoons olive
- 1 onion
- 3 ribs celery
- 1 carrot
- 3 bay leaves
- ¼ tsp dried marjoram
- ½ tsp salt
- black pepper
- 2 cloves garlic
- 14-ounces cod fish
- 14-ounces yams
- 2 anchovy filets
- 4 cups water
- ½ lemon

DIRECTIONS

1. In a pot place olive oil over medium heat and add the onions, cook for 3-4 minutes
2. Add carrots, yams and celery and cook for 4-5 minutes

3. Add bay leaves, anchovies, lemon juice, water, marjoram and salt
4. Add the garlic and cook for 30-40 minutes
5. Add the fish and cook for 15-20 minutes, when is ready remove and serve

CUCUMBER SOUP

Serves: 6

Prep Time: 10 Minutes

Cook Time: 60 Minutes

Total Time: 70 Minutes

INGREDIENTS

- 2 tsp butter
- ¼ tsp salt
- 1/8 tsp pepper
- ¾ cup sour cream
- ½ yogurt
- fresh dill
- 2 cucumbers
- 3 cups low sodium chicken
- ¼ white wine
- 1 tablespoon fresh dill

DIRECTIONS

1. In a skillet add butter over medium heat
2. Add cucumber and chicken and sauté for 5-10 minutes, boil and stir and add wine
3. Let it simmer for 5-10 minutes and add pepper and dill
4. Blend until smooth using a blender and let it cool
5. Add ½ cup of sour cream and yogurt and whisk until smooth, serve with sour cream

CHICKPEA SOUP

Serves: *4*

Prep Time: *10* Minutes

Cook Time: *60* Minutes

Total Time: *70* Minutes

INGREDIENTS

- 2-quarts water
- 3-ounces celery
- 3-ounces carrots
- 2 cups vegetable stock
- 1 cup water
- 3 ounces dried lentils
- 3-ounces chickpeas
- 2 tsp olive oil
- ¼ tsp salt
- 2 bay leaves

DIRECTIONS

1. In a large bowl place the lentils, chickpeas and water and let it stand for 11-12 hours, then drain and set aside
2. In a saucepan add olive oil over medium heat
3. Add celery and carrots and cook for 5-10 minutes
4. Add water, bay leaves, vegetable stock, lentils and chickpeas
5. Reduce the heat to low and simmer for 40-45 minutes

6. Add pepper and salt if needed and cook for a couple of more minutes
7. Serve when ready

LENTIL CHILI

Serves: **4**

Prep Time: **10** Minutes

Cook Time: **60** Minutes

Total Time: **70** Minutes

INGREDIENTS

- 2 tablespoons olive oil
- 2 cloves garlic
- 4 cups water
- 1 cup lentils
- 5 tablespoons sour cream
- 5 ounces reduced-fat cheese
- 1 onion
- 1 15-ounce can tomatoes
- 1 tablespoon chili powder
- 1 tsp ground cumin
- 2 tsp dried oregano
- ¼ chipotle pepper
- ½ tsp salt
- black pepper

DIRECTIONS

1. In a saucepan add olive oil over medium heat
2. Add onion and garlic and cook, add tomatoes, oregano, chipotle, cumin, salt, chili powder and stir

3. Add water and lentils and reduce heat and simmer for 50-60 minutes
4. Serve with sour cream and reduced fat cheese

POTAGE A LA FLORENTINE

Serves: **6**

Prep Time: **10** Minutes

Cook Time: **60** Minutes

Total Time: **70** Minutes

INGREDIENTS

- 1-ounce butter
- ¼ cup onions
- 1 lb. spinach
- 3 tablespoons flour
- 3 cups chicken
- 1 cup water
- 1 tsp nutmeg
- ¼ tsp salt
- ½ cup sherry
- 2 cups milk
- ½ cup brown rice

DIRECTIONS

1. **In a stock pot melt the butter over medium heat, add onion, spinach and cook for 3-4 minutes**
2. **Add flour, chicken stock and cook for 4-5 minutes**
3. **Add rice and cook, soup will thicken**
4. **Add nutmeg, salt, sherry and cook for 4-5 minutes**

CHICKEN NOODLE SOUP

Serves: **4**

Prep Time: **10** Minutes

Cook Time: **40** Minutes

Total Time: **50** Minutes

INGREDIENTS

- 1 tsp olive oil
- 1 onion
- 2 ribs celery
- 2 carrots
- 2 cups chicken broths
- ½ tsp salt
- 1 lb. chicken thighs
- black pepper
- ¼ dried tarragon
- 3-quarts water
- 5-ounces noodles
- 1 tablespoon fresh parsley

DIRECTIONS

1. In a sauce pan add one olive oil over medium heat
2. Add chicken and cook on low heat and remove it
3. Add onion, celery and cook for 5-10 minutes
4. Add carrots, chicken stock, chicken, salt, tarragon and water
5. Reduce the heat and simmer for 40-45 minutes

6. Let it boil for 5-10 minutes and add noodles
7. Drain the noodles and serve with parsley

CHICKEN NOODLE SOUP – COUMADIN SAFE

Serves: **4**

Prep Time: **10** Minutes

Cook Time: **40** Minutes

Total Time: **50** Minutes

INGREDIENTS

- 1 tsp olive oil
- 1 lb. chicken thighs
- 1 onion
- 2 ribs celery
- 2 carrots
- 2 cups chicken broths
- black pepper
- ¼ dried tarragon
- 3-quarts water
- 5-ounces noodles
- 1 tablespoon fresh parsley

DIRECTIONS

1. In a sauce pan add one olive oil over medium heat
2. Add chicken and cook on low heat and remove it
3. Add onion, celery and cook for 5-10 minutes
4. Add carrots, chicken stock, chicken, tarragon and water
5. Reduce the heat and simmer for 40-45 minutes

6. Let it boil for 5-10 minutes and add noodles
7. Drain the noodles and serve with parsley

ROASTED EGGPLANT SOUP

Serves: **4**

Prep Time: **10** Minutes

Cook Time: **100** Minutes

Total Time: **110** Minutes

INGREDIENTS

- ¼ lb. plum tomatoes
- 1 ½ lbs. eggplant
- ½ lb shallots
- 5 cloves garlic
- 2 tsp dried thyme
- 3 cups chicken broth
- ¼ cup wine
- 1 cup water
- ½ tsp salt
- 1 cup milk

DIRECTIONS

1. Preheat oven to 375 F
2. Spray a roasting pan with olive oil and place all the vegetables there
3. Roast for 40-45 minutes
4. Remove them from the oven and let cool
5. Scoop the eggplant

6. Add to the pot the roasted vegetables, chicken stock, wine, thyme and water
7. Reduce the heat to low and simmer for 40-45 minutes
8. Stir in milk
9. Remove when ready and serve

ROASTED TOMATO SOUP WITH GARLIC

Serves: **4**

Prep Time: **10** Minutes

Cook Time: **130** Minutes

Total Time: **140** Minutes

INGREDIENTS

- 2 lbs. tomatoes
- 1 tsp olive oil
- 1 tablespoon rosemary
- 1 tablespoon thyme
- ½ tsp red pepper flakes
- 3 2-ounce whole wheat
- 1 fresh corn
- 1/3 cups onion
- 2 cloves garlic
- 1 cup chicken broth
- 2 cups water
- ¼ cups wine

DIRECTIONS

1. **Preheat oven to 400F**
2. **Spray a roasting pan with olive oil and add the tomatoes**
3. **Place the pan in the oven for 50-60 minutes**
4. **Slice the corn in a sauce pan and let it boil for 5-10 minutes and then remove it**

5. Heat olive oil in pot over medium heat and add onion, corn and cook, stir frequently
6. Add garlic and stir for 2-3 minutes
7. Remove the tomatoes and blend them in a blender
8. Place the mixture over medium heat and add the tomato
9. Add wine, rosemary, water chicken stock and red pepper flakes
10. Cook for 15-20 minutes and serve with whole wheat

ROASTED YAM SOUP

Serves: 4

Prep Time: 10 Minutes

Cook Time: 50 Minutes

Total Time: 60 Minutes

INGREDIENTS

- 1 lb. yams
- 2 tsp olive oil
- ¼ tsp salt
- 3 strips bacon
- 1 cup milk
- black pepper
- 1 onion
- 1 tablespoon dried sage
- 1/3 tsp dried peppermint
- 1 cup chicken broth
- 1 cup water

DIRECTIONS

1. Preheat oven to 300 F and place the yam to bake for 30-40 minutes
2. Remove and let cool for 5-10 minutes
3. In a saucepan add olive oil over medium heat, add onions and cook for 4-5 minutes
4. Add chicken stock, water, peppermint, sage, salt and pepper and cook for 30-35 minutes

5. Slice the yams and add the flesh to the pan, cook for 5-10 minutes
6. Add milk and then puree until smooth and reduce the heat
7. In a skillet add bacon over medium heat, cool until crispy
8. Slice the yams and add to the pan, cook for 5-10 minutes
9. Add to the soup and serve

ROASTED YAM SOUP – LOW SODIUM

Serves: **4**

Prep Time: **10** Minutes

Cook Time: **50** Minutes

Total Time: **60** Minutes

INGREDIENTS

- 1 lb. yams
- 2 tsp olive oil
- 3 strips bacon
- 1 cup milk
- black pepper
- 1 onion
- 1 tablespoon dried sage
- 1/3 tsp dried peppermint
- 1 cup chicken broth
- 1 cup water

DIRECTIONS

1. Preheat oven to 300 F and place the yam to bake for 30-40 minutes
2. Remove and let cool for 5-10 minutes
3. In a saucepan add olive oil over medium heat, add onions and cook for 4-5 minutes
4. Add chicken stock, water, peppermint, sage and pepper and cook for 30-35 minutes
5. Slice the yams and add the flesh to the pan, cook for 5-10 minutes

6. Add milk and then puree until smooth and reduce the heat
7. In a skillet add bacon over medium heat, cool until crispy
8. Slice the yams and add to the pan, cook for 5-10 minutes
9. Add to the soup and serve

BEAN SOUP

Serves: **4**

Prep Time: **10** Minutes

Cook Time: **230** Minutes

Total Time: **240** Minutes

INGREDIENTS

- 2 cups beans
- 1/2 tsp salt
- 2 cups chicken broth
- 7 cups water
- 2 tsp sauce
- ½ 10-ounce package onions
- 2 clove garlic
- 3 bay leaves
- ½ tsp dried rosemary
- 1 tsp dried sage
- 2 tsp dried thyme

DIRECTIONS

1. Place the bean mixture in a pot with the rest of ingredients
2. Cook over medium heat until the soup boils
3. Reduce the heat and simmer for 3-4 hours
4. When ready remove from heat and serve

WHITE BEAN SOUP

Serves: *6*

Prep Time: *10* Minutes

Cook Time: *80* Minutes

Total Time: *90* Minutes

INGREDIENTS

- 3 quarts-water
- 3 ribs celery
- 3 carrots
- ¾ tsp salt
- black pepper
- 2 1/2 lbs. leftover turkey meat
- 3 15-ounce can white beans
- 1 tablespoon dried sage

DIRECTIONS

1. In a pot place water over high heat, add turkey and boil for 25-30 minutes
2. Add broth to the pot with the white beans, carrots, celery, turkey meat and pepper
3. Simmer for 90 minutes over medium heat
4. Remove and serve

WHITE BEAN SOUP WITH KALE

Serves: *4*

Prep Time: *10* Minutes

Cook Time: *50* Minutes

Total Time: *60* Minutes

INGREDIENTS

- 1 tsp olive oil
- 10-ounces kale
- 1-ounce pancetta
- 1 onion
- 1 carrot
- 2 15 ounces can white beans
- 3 cups water
- 1 tsp dried marjoram
- ¼ tsp salt
- black pepper
- 1 tsp maple syrup

DIRECTIONS

1. Slice the kale in half
2. In a skillet ad one teaspoon of olive oil and add the kale and cook for 5-10 minutes
3. Remove from the pan and add ham and cook for 2-3 minutes
4. Add the carrots and onion and cook for 5-6 minutes

5. Add the salt, pepper, maple syrup, water and beans
6. Reduce the heat and simmer for 25-30 minutes
7. When ready remove and let it cool

WHITE BEAN CHILI

Serves: **6**

Prep Time: **10** Minutes

Cook Time: **50** Minutes

Total Time: **60** Minutes

INGREDIENTS

- 2 15-ounce can white beans
- 2 tablespoons canola oil
- ¼ tsp salt
- 1 tsp ground cumin
- ¼ cup milk
- 3-ounces cheddar cheese
- 3 tsp sour cream
- 1 tablespoon cilantro leaves
- 2 small onions
- 1 clove garlic
- 1 lb. russet potatoes
- 2 cups chicken broth
- 1 ½ cups wine
- 2 ½ cups water
- 1 ½ lb. chicken breast

DIRECTIONS

1. **Rinse the beans with water**
2. **In a pot add oil over medium heat**

3. Add garlic and onion and cook, add potatoes, chicken stock and wine
4. Cook on low heat for 25-30 minutes
5. Add chicken, cumin and beans and stir
6. Add cheese and milk and stir
7. Serve with 2 teaspoons of sour cream and 1 tablespoon cilantro leaves

SOUP

CHICKEN WONTON SOUP

Serves: **10**

Prep Time: **20** Minutes

Cook Time: **60** Minutes

Total Time: **80** Minutes

INGREDIENTS

- 3 tablespoons olive oil
- 1 onion
- 1 tablespoon red wine vinegar
- ¼ red pepper flakes
- 14 mushrooms caps
- 5 carrots
- 1 cup shelled edamame
- 4 scallions
- 1 tablespoon grated ginger
- 1 clove garlic
- 1 ½ lbs. chicken
- 40 wonton wrappers
- 11 cups water
- ¾ tsp salt
- ½ tsp black pepper

DIRECTIONS

1. In a pan heat olive oil over medium heat, add onion, garlic and ginger and cook for 5-10 minutes
2. Add salt and chicken to the pan
3. Brush a shallow dish with water and add a linked baking sheet, fold into a triangle tip, roll into the bottom of the wrapper
4. Combine water, salt, pepper, vinegar in pot and boil, add mushrooms, carrots, edamame and let it cook for 20-25 minutes
5. Serve sprinkled with scallions

HOMEMADE CHICKEN NUGGETS

Serves: **4**

Prep Time: **10** Minutes

Cook Time: **30** Minutes

Total Time: **40** Minutes

INGREDIENTS

- 1 lbs. chicken breast
- 2 small eggs
- ¼ tsp garlic powder
- ¼ tsp salt
- ¼ cup breadcrumbs
- 1 ½ cups cauliflower

DIRECTIONS

1. Preheat oven to 325 F and place a baking tray in
2. In a bowl mix garlic powder, salt and egg and whisk together
3. In another bowl mix cauliflower and breadcrumbs, dip the chicken into the mixture
4. Bake for 20-25 minutes on each side

ROASTED VEGGIE BREAKFAST TACOS

Serves: **4**

Prep Time: **10** Minutes

Cook Time: **10** Minutes

Total Time: **20** Minutes

INGREDIENTS

- 2 sweet potatoes
- 1 carrot
- 2 tablespoons olive oil
- 1 tsp ground cumin
- ¼ coriander
- ½ tsp salt
- zest of ½ lime
- 1 cup black beans
- 2 tortillas

DIRECTIONS

1. Preheat oven to 325 F and line a baking sheet with parchment paper
2. In a bowl mix carrot, olive oil, sweet potatoes, coriander, cumin and lime zest, move everything on the baking sheet
3. Roast for 15-20 minutes and when ready spread the black beans on the tortilla and top with vegetables
4. Serve when ready

PUDDING WITH HONEYDEW MELON

Serves: **2**

Prep Time: **10** Minutes

Cook Time: **230** Minutes

Total Time: **240** Minutes

INGREDIENTS

- 1 cup soy milk
- ½ cup chia seeds
- ½ cup honeydew melon

DIRECTIONS

1. In a bowl mix chia seed and soy milk
2. Cover and transfer to the refrigerator for 2 and a half hours
3. Remove and top with melon before serving

ROASTED VEGGIE WITH CHEESE

Serves: **4**

Prep Time: **10** Minutes

Cook Time: **30** Minutes

Total Time: **40** Minutes

INGREDIENTS

- 1/4 zucchini
- 2 tsp oregano
- 1 tablespoon olive oil
- 3 eggs
- ¼ tsp turmeric
- ¼ cup goat cheese
- ¼ cup broccoli florets
- 1 carrot
- ¼ sweet potato
- ½ cup Bella mushrooms
- 1 tsp basil
- ¼ tsp thyme

DIRECTIONS

1. **Preheat oven to 325 F**
2. **Add the vegetables in a pan with oregano and olive oil and roast for 20-25 minutes**
3. **In another bowl whisk together turmeric, goat cheese and eggs**
4. **Remove vegetables from the oven and pour the egg mixture over them**

SWEET POTATO WITH GINGER-HONEY ALMOND BUTTER

Serves: 2

Prep Time: 10 Minutes

Cook Time: 10 Minutes

Total Time: 20 Minutes

INGREDIENTS

- 1 sweet potato
- ¼ tsp ginger
- 1 kiwi
- 2 tablespoons almond butter
- ¼ tsp honey

DIRECTIONS

1. In a bowl stir ginger, honey and almond butter together
2. Slice sweet potato in into ¼ inch slices
3. Toast the sweet potato until soft
4. Spread one side of each potato slide with almond mixture

APPLE CARROT MUFFINS

Serves: **10**

Prep Time: **10** Minutes

Cook Time: **40** Minutes

Total Time: **50** Minutes

INGREDIENTS

- 1 cup whole wheat flour
- ½ cup sugar
- 2 tablespoons olive oil
- ½ cup Greek yogurt
- ¼ up applesauce
- 3 carrots
- ¼ fresh cranberries
- ¼ baking powder
- ¼ tsp baking soda
- 1 tsp cinnamon
- ¼ tsp salt
- 1 cup oats
- 1 tablespoon flaxseed
- 2 tablespoons water

DIRECTIONS

1. **Preheat oven to 374 F and spray a 12 cup muffin tin with cooking spray**

2. Whisk together the baking powder, baking soda, flour, sugar, oats, salt and cinnamon and stir
3. Add yogurt, applesauce and yogurt and whisk together
4. Add cranberries and carrots, spoon the batter among the muffin tin and bake for 25-30 minutes
5. When ready, remove and let it cool

DRIED PERSIMMON ROUNDS

Serves: **4**

Prep Time: **10** Minutes

Cook Time: **110** Minutes

Total Time: **120** Minutes

INGREDIENTS

- 5 large Fuyu persimmons

DIRECTIONS

1. Preheat oven to 275 F
2. Slice the persimmons into ¼ inch rounds
3. Divide the persimmons between 2 wire racks
4. Bake until looks dry for 1 ½ hours
5. Remove and serve

PAPAYA YOGURT

Serves: 2

Prep Time: 5 Minutes

Cook Time: 10 Minutes

Total Time: 15 Minutes

INGREDIENTS

- 1 papaya
- ½ cup walnuts
- ½ teaspoon ground cinnamon
- ¼ Greek yogurt

DIRECTIONS

1. Scoop out the seeds of the papaya
2. Fill each papaya with walnut halves, yogurt
3. Sprinkle with cinnamon
4. Serve when ready

BERRY ICE CUBES WITH SELTZER

Serves: **2**

Prep Time: **5** Minutes

Cook Time: **5** Minutes

Total Time: **10** Minutes

INGREDIENTS

- ½ cup blueberries
- ½ cup blackberries
- water
- setzer water
- ½ cup raspberries

DIRECTIONS

1. Divide the berries into 16 cube ice cube tray
2. Add water and store to refrigerator
3. Serve with setzer water

DIY BAGELS

Serves: **6**

Prep Time: **40** Minutes

Cook Time: **80** Minutes

Total Time: **120** Minutes

INGREDIENTS

- 1 cup water
- 1 packet active yeast
- 1 egg
- 1 tablespoon sugar
- 3 cups bread flour
- 2 ½ tsp salt

DIRECTIONS

1. In a bowl whisk together yeast, sugar and water
2. In a food processor mix flour and salt, add yeast mixture and mix for 5-10 minutes
3. Transfer dough to a bowl, cover for one hour
4. In a pot, boil water and preheat the oven to 400 F
5. Transfer the dough and divide into 8 equal sized pieces
6. Roll each piece into a ball
7. Place 4 bagels in the water and cook for 1-2 minutes, remove when ready
8. Combine a tablespoon of water with egg and whisk, brush with egg wash

9. Bake for 15-20 minutes
10. Remove and let it cool

GRILLED VEGETABLES

Serves: **4**

Prep Time: **10** Minutes

Cook Time: **10** Minutes

Total Time: **20** Minutes

INGREDIENTS

- 1 tablespoon olive oil
- ¼ tsp salt
- 2 bell peppers
- 1 bunch asparagus
- 2 small zucchini
- 1 tablespoon rice vinegar
- 1 tablespoon oregano
- 1 eggplant

DIRECTIONS

1. In a bowl whisk salt, oregano, vinegar and olive oil
2. Place the vegetables into a bowl
3. Place vegetables on a grill
4. Cook eggplant and zucchini pieces for 5-6 minutes per side
5. Toss asparagus and cool for 4-5 minutes
6. Transfer to a plate and serve when ready

APPLE CRISP DESSET

Serves: **4**

Prep Time: **20** Minutes

Cook Time: **30** Minutes

Total Time: **50** Minutes

INGREDIENTS

- 3 apples
- 1 tsp cornstarch
- 1 tsp cinnamon
- 1 tablespoon brown sugar
- ¼ teaspoon salt
- ½ walnuts
- 5 tablespoons apple juice
- ¼ lemon
- ½ tsp lemon zest
- 1 tablespoons sugar
- 2 tablespoons butter
- 2 tablespoons flour
- ¼ oats

DIRECTIONS

1. **Preheat oven to 325 F and spray ramekins with cooking spray**
2. **In a bowl combine cinnamon, lemon juice, apples, lemon juice, sugar and lemon zest**

3. In another bowl combine brown sugar, salt, flour, butter, walnuts and oats and mix well
4. Spoon the mixture into ramekins, top each serving with apple juice
5. Bake for 25-30 minutes, remove and serve

BUTTERMILK RANCH DRESSING

Serves: **4**

Prep Time: **10** Minutes

Cook Time: **30** Minutes

Total Time: **40** Minutes

INGREDIENTS

- ¼ cup buttermilk
- ½ cup mayonnaise
- ½ cup Greek yogurt
- 1 tablespoons chives
- 1 tablespoon parsley
- 1 tablespoon lemon juice
- 1 teaspoon lemon zest
- 1 tsp garlic powder
- 1 tsp salt
- ¼ tsp black pepper

DIRECTIONS

1. In a bowl combine mayo, Greek yogurt and buttermilk, add chopped parsley, chives, garlic powder, lemon zest, salt, lemon juice and pepper
2. Whisk everything and place in the refrigerator

PESTO AND BUTTERNUT SQUASH PIZZA

Serves: **6**

Prep Time: **10** Minutes

Cook Time: **130** Minutes

Total Time: **140** Minutes

INGREDIENTS

- 1 package active yeast
- 3 tablespoons Parmesan cheese
- 1 ¼ cup water
- 1 ½ cup whole wheat flour
- 1 cup flour
- 1 tsp salt
- 2 tsp sugar
- 1 tablespoon olive oil
- 1 cup butternut squash
- 2 tablespoons prepared pesto
- ¼ cup skim mozzarella cheese

DIRECTIONS

1. In a bowl mix sugar, water and yeast and stir
2. For dough mix flour and salt in a bowl, add yeast mixture and olive oil
3. When ready transfer to an oiled bowl and let it rise for one hour
4. Preheat oven to 375 F and prepare a sheet pan with parchment paper

5. Add butternut squash on the sheet pan and roast
6. Transfer dough to pan and top with pesto
7. Bake for 15-20 minutes at 425 F, when is golden brown remove and let it cool

CRISPY FRENCH FRIES

Serves: **4**

Prep Time: **10** Minutes

Cook Time: **30** Minutes

Total Time: **40** Minutes

INGREDIENTS

- 3 russet potatoes
- ¼ tsp salt
- ½ tsp black pepper
- 1 tablespoon olive oil

DIRECTIONS

1. Preheat oven to 375 F and line a baking sheet with parchment paper
2. Slice the potatoes and cut into small pieces
3. Transfer to the baking sheet and bake for 30-35 minutes
4. When golden brown, remove from the oven and let them cool

MANGO COLESLAW

Serves: **4**

Prep Time: **10** Minutes

Cook Time: **30** Minutes

Total Time: **40** Minutes

INGREDIENTS

- ½ cup rice vinegar
- 1 tablespoons canola oil
- 1 tsp sugar
- ¼ tsp celery seed
- ¼ tsp salt
- 3 cups green cabbage
- 2 cups carrots
- 1 cup fresh mango

DIRECTIONS

1. In a bowl whisk oil, sugar, celery seeds, vinegar and salt
2. Add carrots, mango and cabbage
3. Toss all the ingredients in the dressing and store to the refrigerator

CHICKEN WITH TURMERIC

Serves: **4**

Prep Time: **10** Minutes

Cook Time: **30** Minutes

Total Time: **40** Minutes

INGREDIENTS

- 2 ½ tsp olive oil
- ½ tsp salt
- 3 chicken breasts
- 2 tsp ground turmeric
- ¼ tsp fennel seed

DIRECTIONS

1. Preheat oven to 350 F and line a baking sheet with parchment paper
2. In a bowl mix turmeric, salt, fennel and oil
3. Place the chicken breast on the baking sheet and brush with the mixture
4. Transfer to the oven and bake for 25-30 minutes
5. Remove and let it cool before serving

WILD BLUEBERRY MUFFINS

Serves: **10**
Prep Time: **10** Minutes
Cook Time: **20** Minutes
Total Time: **30** Minutes

INGREDIENTS

- 2 cups whole wheat flour
- ¼ cup sugar
- ½ cup Greek Yogurt
- 2 eggs
- 1 tsp vanilla extract
- 1 cup wild blueberries
- ¼ tablespoon baking soda
- 1 tablespoon lemon zest
- 1 cup almond milk

DIRECTIONS

1. Preheat the oven to 375 F and spray a muffin tin with spray
2. In a bowl whisk together sugar, baking powder, flour and lemon zest
3. Pour the mixture into dry ingredients and stir
4. In another bowl toss blueberry with flour, scoop batter into muffin tin and bake for 20-25 minutes
5. Remove and let it cool before serving

QUINOA SALAD

Serves: 2

Prep Time: 10 Minutes

Cook Time: 10 Minutes

Total Time: 20 Minutes

INGREDIENTS

- 2 cup asparagus spears
- ¼ cup peas
- 1/3 cup fresh mint leaves
- 1 lemon juiced
- 2 tablespoons olive oil
- 1/3 tsp black pepper
- 1 cup quinoa
- 2 ½ cups arugula
- ¼ cup radishes

DIRECTIONS

1. In a skillet place asparagus and peas and bring to boil
2. Remove from heat and it cool and drain
3. In a bowl toss asparagus, quinoa, radishes, peas, arugula and mint
4. In a bowl whisk together olive oil, pepper and lemon juice and pour over salad
5. Refrigerate before serving

OVERNIGHT OATMEAL

Serves: **4**

Prep Time: **10** Minutes

Cook Time: **30** Minutes

Total Time: **40** Minutes

INGREDIENTS

- 1 cup skim milk
- 1 tsp vanilla
- ¼ rolled oats
- ½ cup banana
- ½ cup Greek yogurt
- 1 tsp honey

DIRECTIONS

1. In a jar whisk together yogurt, honey, milk, oats and vanilla
2. Cover and refrigerate overnight
3. Serve in the morning with banana

AVOCADO CHICKEN SALAD

Serves: **4**

Prep Time: **10** Minutes

Cook Time: **30** Minutes

Total Time: **40** Minutes

INGREDIENTS

- 1 chicken breast
- garlic powder
- 1 tsp lemon juice
- ½ cup diced onion
- ½ cup celery
- black pepper
- 1 small avocado
- 1 tsp Greek yogurt

DIRECTIONS

1. **Preheat oven to 325 F**
2. **Season chicken breast with pepper and garlic powder and bake for 30-35 minutes**
3. **Remove and let it cool**
4. **In a bowl mix lime juice, avocado, garlic powder and pepper, stir in chicken and onion and store in the refrigerator**

BASIL FARRO SALAD

Serves: 2

Prep Time: *10* Minutes

Cook Time: *10* Minutes

Total Time: *20* Minutes

INGREDIENTS

- 2 cups cooked faro
- 2 tablespoons olive oil
- 1 tablespoon balsamic vinegar
- 2 clove garlic
- 1 1⁄2 cup cherry tomatoes
- ½ cup basil leaves
- ½ cup mozzarella

DIRECTIONS

1. In a bowl mixt tomatoes, basil, farro and mozzarella
2. In another bowl whisk together the rest of the ingredients and pour over farro mixture
3. Serve immediately or refrigerate

STRAWBERRY ICE CUBES

Serves: **4**

Prep Time: **10** Minutes

Cook Time: **230** Minutes

Total Time: **240** Minutes

INGREDIENTS

- 2 green tea bags
- 1 ½ tablespoons honey
- 1 cup strawberries
- 2 cups water

DIRECTIONS

1. Heat water, brew tea and mix in honey and stir
2. Allow to cool and pour the mixture into ice cube tray
3. Place everything into the refrigerator
4. Once frozen remove and serve

LEMON ZUCCHINI SALAD

Serves: **4**

Prep Time: **10** Minutes

Cook Time: **10** Minutes

Total Time: **20** Minutes

INGREDIENTS

- 2 small zucchini
- 2 cups green peas
- 2 cups beans
- 1 tablespoon dill
- zest from 1 lemon
- ¼ tsp salt

DIRECTIONS

1. **In a bowl combine all the ingredients**
2. **Serve when ready**

SPICED CHICKEN AND VEGETABLE SOUP

Serves: *4*

Prep Time: *10* Minutes

Cook Time: *50* Minutes

Total Time: *60* Minutes

INGREDIENTS

- 2 skinless chicken breast
- 1 tablespoon cumin
- 1 carrot
- 1 14-ounce can white beans
- 1 zucchini
- 1 cup kale
- 1 tsp oregano
- ¼ tsp salt
- 1/3 cup barley

DIRECTIONS

1. Boil 8 cups of water and add cumin, oregano, chicken breast and salt
2. Boil for 15-20 minutes
3. Remove the chicken and save the liquid
4. Add barley and boil for 15-20 minutes
5. Add beans, carrots and cook for 15-20 minutes
6. Stir in kale, chicken and zucchini
7. Stir for 5 minutes and serve

QUINOA STUFFED CHICKEN ROLL-UPS

Serves: **4**

Prep Time: **10** Minutes

Cook Time: **40** Minutes

Total Time: **50** Minutes

INGREDIENTS

- 1 ½ tablespoons quinoa
- ¼ carrot
- 1/3 tsp oregano
- ½ cup spinach
- 2 ½ tablespoons feta cheese
- zest from ½ lemon
- 1/3 cup broccoli stalks
- 1 chicken breast
- 1/3 tsp salt

DIRECTIONS

1. Steam the broccoli and carrots until tender
2. Preheat oven to 325 F
3. Lay chicken breast on a baking sheet and spray with olive oil
4. In a bowl mixt oregano, quinoa, feta cheese, lemon zest, spinach and chicken breast
5. Begin to roll from one end of the breast until end up with a full roll
6. Transfer the chicken rolls to a pan and cook for 5-10 minutes

7. Transfer the rolls to the oven and cook for 15-20 minutes
8. When ready remove the chicken and let it cool

TURKEY AND MUSHROOM BURGERS

Serves: **4**

Prep Time: **10** Minutes

Cook Time: **30** Minutes

Total Time: **40** Minutes

INGREDIENTS

- ¾ pound turkey breast
- 2 tablespoons olive oil
- 1 tablespoons sauce
- 1/3 cup Bella mushrooms

DIRECTIONS

1. In a bowl mix turkey breast, olive oil, sauce and mushrooms
2. Divide the mixture into 4 parts
3. Grease a skillet with oil and cook each side for 5-6 minutes

LEMON-ZESTED SHRIMP

Serves: 2
Prep Time: 10 Minutes
Cook Time: 5 Minutes
Total Time: 15 Minutes

INGREDIENTS

- 6 medium shrimp
- 1/3 tsp olive oil
- 1 tsp cilantro
- 2 slices whole wheat bread
- 1/3 medium avocado
- ¼ mango
- ¼ tsp lemon zest
- 1/6 cumin

DIRECTIONS

1. In a bowl mix olive oil, cumin, lemon zest, shrimp and cilantro
2. Heat a frying pan and add the shrimp, cook for 5-6 minutes each side
3. Toast the whole wheat bread and mash the avocado
4. Spread the avocado mash over the toasted bread
5. Top with mango sliced and shrimp

COD PARCHMENT PACKS

Serves: **4**

Prep Time: **10** Minutes

Cook Time: **30** Minutes

Total Time: **40** Minutes

INGREDIENTS

- 2 1/2 cups sweet potato
- 1 pound cod
- 3 tsp olive oil
- 2 tsp salt
- 3 slices of lemon
- 1 tsp thyme leaves

DIRECTIONS

1. Preheat oven to 375 F and fold 4 sheets of parchment paper in half
2. Place sweet potatoes on the parchment paper and sprinkle each side of fish with olive oil, thyme and salt
3. Fold the parchment paper over the fish
4. Transfer everything to a baking sheet and bake for 15-20 minutes
5. Remove and let it cool before serving

PANCACKES WITH RED APPLES

Serves: **4**

Prep Time: **10** Minutes

Cook Time: **20** Minutes

Total Time: **30** Minutes

INGREDIENTS

- ½ cup whole wheat flour
- ¼ cup flour
- 1 tablespoon sugar
- 2 tablespoons butter
- 2 red apples
- ¼ tsp ginger
- 1 tablespoons water
- 1 tsp honey
- 1 tsp baking powder
- 1/3 tsp salt
- 1 cup milk
- 1 egg
- 3 tablespoons avocado
- 1 tablespoon water

DIRECTIONS

1. **In a bowl combine the dry ingredients**

2. In another bowl whisk together the wet ingredients and stir well
3. Spray a pan with oil and spoon the pancake batter into the pan, cook for 4-5 minutes each side
4. In a bowl pour the butter over apple slices
5. Arrange the pancakes on a plate and sprinkle with honey

CHICKEN SOUP NOODLE BOWL

Serves: **2**

Prep Time: **10** Minutes

Cook Time: **10** Minutes

Total Time: **20** Minutes

INGREDIENTS

- 2 cups chicken broth
- 1 ounce rice noodles
- ½ cup sugar snap peas
- 2 ounces shredded chicken

DIRECTIONS

1. In a sauce pan heat chicken broth and add rice noodles, stir frequently
2. Add snap peas and cook chicken for 4-5 minutes until peas are tender
3. Serve when ready

Made in the USA
Coppell, TX
01 July 2021